THE 21 LAWS OF STRIP CLUB ECONOMICS

Darius Allen has a degree in economics from the University of Southern California. He advocates that you should always visit a gentlemen's club with an agenda and a healthy attitude.

THE 21 LAWS

The 21 Laws of Surviving a Gentlemen's Club
The 21Laws of Being an Exotic Dancer
The 21 Laws of Being a Bikini Barista

www.the21laws.com

THE 21 LAWS OF STRIP CLUB ECONOMICS

Darius Allen

Varsity Club

Copyright © 2019 by Darius Allen

All rights reserved
No part of this book may be reproduced or transmitted in any form or by any means, electronic or mechanical, including photocopying, recording, or by any information storage and retrieval system, without permission in writing from the publisher.

PUBLISHED BY VARSITY CLUB PUBLISHING
a division of Varsity Club Enterprises, LLC.

Varsity Club

is a registered trademark of Varsity Club Enterprises, LLC.
Manufactured and printed in the United States of America
Library of Congress Cataloging in Publication Data

The 21 Laws of Strip Club Economics/Darius Allen
1. Economics 2. Business & Money
3. Humor & Entertainment
4. Sex

ISBN: 978-0-9974320-9-1

Cover design and Illustrations by Jesse Gonzales
Edited by Trojans

THIS BOOK IS DEDICATED TO THOSE PATRONS WHO TRULY APPRECIATE THE ENTERTAINMENT VALUE THAT A CLASSICAL OR OTHERWISE NEOCLASSICAL STRIP CLUB HAS TO OFFER.

NEVER FORGET THAT YOU ARE VITAL TO THE CONTINUAL GROWTH AND STABILITY OF THE STRIP CLUB INDUSTRY.
BEST BELIEVE, YOU ARE VALUED.

TABLE OF CONTENTS

The Economist Note

Hearing the title 'economist' will throw most strip club enthusiasts for a loop. The very mention of the title evokes the image of a square in a modest suit, with a white button-up shirt and a striped tie—a combo that you can find straight off the Nordstrom clearance rack—and a trademark pair of black frames. Nothing flashy and not someone you would associate with "making it rain." Or one can picture a middle-aged woman wearing a conservative dress, plain jane heels (no red bottoms) and modest jewelry, giving a lecture about wealth inequality—again—nothing about getting "lit" and caressing the backside of a sexy stripper with tiger stripes.

According to Merriam-Webster.com:

economist

noun econ·o·mist \ i-ˈkä-nə-mist \

1 *archaic*: one who practices economy

2 : a specialist in economics

Okay, that definition is almost as boring as the mere utterance of the word. But how does the title apply to the strip club? In Strip Club Economics 101, an economist is a patron who is:

Efficient	- You're capable of sticking to your agenda.
Calculating	- You're unapologetically shrewd with your time and money.
Optimistic	- You positively welcome the entertainment value provided by the strip club.
Noble	- You're an avid investor in the strip club industry.
Opportunistic	- You gladly take advantage of opportunities that arise.
Mobile	- You keep it moving, adapting and adjusting to the market.
Intuitive	- You understand the power of intuition.
Sexual	- You're in tune with your sexual nature and unquenchable thirst.
Timely	- You're conscious of your time as a limited resource.

So, given the acronym, can you now see things from a different angle? Can you relate? If you can, then you already have the mindset to be a **Strip Club Economist**.

Preface

Economics is a subject profoundly conducive to cliche, resonant with boredom. On few topics is an American audience so practiced in turning off its ears and minds. And none can say that the response is ill advised.

—John Kenneth Galbraith

When most people think about the study of economics, the overall consensus is summed up with a quote by famed director and social critic, Michael Moore.

"No one is entertained by economics."

He does have a point.

As an economics major from the University of Southern California, I can certainly understand that statement. For example, I can't remember anything entertaining about Econ 318 (Introduction to Econometrics) and all the statistical methods that came along with it. And for the record, that's the hardest class I've ever taken in my academic life. It was a grueling experience. To this day, I still can't believe I made it out alive with a passing grade.

But, as an economics major, I know that it all depends on how you look at things and where you place your analytical eye. Economics is all around us, and every day is a battleground between limited choices and trade-offs.

There's no escaping the reality of scarcity.

As far as the entertainment factor, that's only lacking because economists are afraid to enter certain environments like the strip club.

The strip club doesn't care about academic status, degrees, and certifications. It's one thing to be called a rogue economist, but entering the darkness of a strip club and discussing the sexual components of supply and demand is a little too rogue for the profession. Playing the strip club game (theory) and experiencing the patron's dilemma brings a whole new level and definition to the already complex world of game theory. It takes courage and rebelliousness to venture into the depths of the jungle, take a seat on a velvet couch, pull out a pen and pad, and observe its capitalistic nature.

This brings us to
The 21 Laws of Strip Club Economics.

Truth be told, all the economic concepts and theories are right there in the club, grasping and clutching at one's ankles like a vulture scraping the main floor. Understand that before you even take your first step into the club, before you even take a seat at the tip rail and drizzle your first dollar bill, you made an <u>economic</u> decision to enter the jungle. Whether that decision was **rational** or **irrational** remains to be seen—but the decision was made.

Seems **rational**, right?

No one is forced to go to a strip club.

The choice is yours.

This introductory book is expressed in a <u>normative economic</u> ("what ought to be") tongue and stated with a <u>positive economic</u> ("what is") outlook—exemplary of the boldness of The 21 Laws collection.

Just like most classical theory-based economists, we make the fundamental assumption that <u>patrons are **rational**</u>, or at least they "ought to be."

Case in point, who in their right mind goes to a strip club to avoid strippers or to talk down on their profession?

That's **irrational**. It doesn't make any sense.

To maximize one's time and money, it is imperative to have an agenda and a **rational** thinking mind.

In strip club economics, **rational** behavior is a mix of common sense, logic, and simplicity. You are there for a reason.

RATIONAL BEHAVIOR

The sole purpose of entering a strip club is to interact (mentality, physically, and financially) with the one and only main attraction, the stripper. Everything else is secondary and a convenient distraction from that fact.

IRRATIONAL BEHAVIOR

Entering a strip club to treat the one and only main attraction, the stripper, as a secondary source of entertainment or a sideshow is irrational and illogical. It goes against the very purpose of a strip club.

The concepts of **rational** behavior and **irrational** behavior have always been at the foundation of economic theory, and as strip clubs continue to evolve from traditional T and A joints to one-stop shops of entertainment, those two concepts will always be driving the conversation.

And the conversation continues…

The 21 Laws of Surviving a Gentlemen's Club put a rare spotlight on the patron's hierarchy of needs (see Fig. 1).

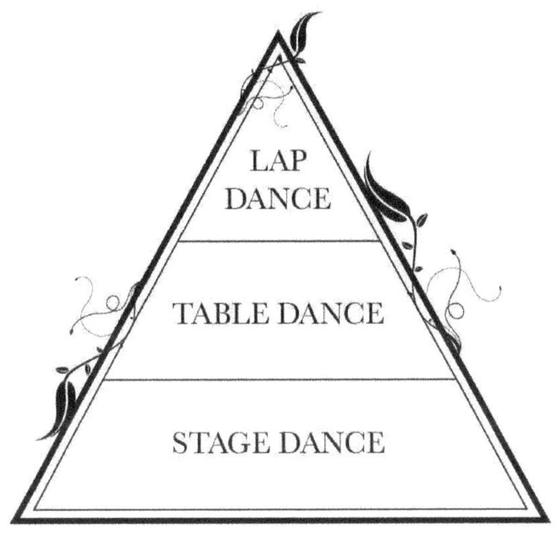

Fig. 1. Patron's Hierarchy of Needs.
From *The 21 Laws of Surviving a Gentlemen's Club* (p. 4), 2017, Varsity Club Publishing.

The 21 Laws of Being an Exotic Dancer discussed the importance of the stripper money cycle (see Fig. 2).

Fig. 2. Stripper Money Cycle.
From *The 21 Laws of Being an Exotic Dancer* (p. 10), 2018, Varsity Club Publishing.

The 21 Laws of Strip Club Economics explores the dynamics of the strip club supply and demand curve and the BANG in the phrase 'Bang for your Buck' (see Fig. 3).

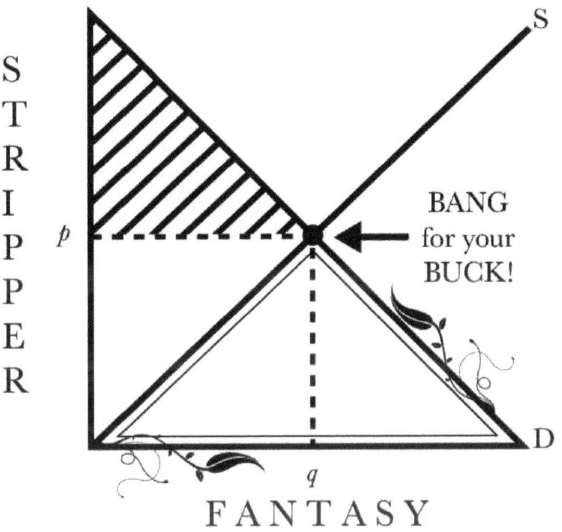

Fig. 3. The Strip Club Supply and Demand Curve.

This one-of-a-kind book intertwines the theories learned in the school of economics and the stripes earned in the jungles of the strip club industry—giving a new twist (and twerk) to the term 'Freakonomics'.

- Laws 1-3: Introduction to Strip Club Economics 101

- Laws 4-6: Understanding Strip Club Economic Theory
- Laws 7-11: Incentives, Demands, and Costs
- Laws 12-17: Micro (G-string) economics 2-4-1
- Laws 18-21: Macro (Industry) economics

It's time to look at economics through a different pair of black frame glasses and show that the only thing lacking is not the entertainment factor, but creativity and imagination. Welcome to *The 21 Laws of Strip Club Economics.*

THE 21 LAWS OF STRIP CLUB ECONOMICS

LAW 1

WHAT IS STRIP CLUB ECONOMICS?

Economics is everywhere, and understanding economics can help you make better decisions and lead a happier life.

—Tyler Cowen

First and foremost, economics is a social science. A strong emphasis is placed on the word *social*. Go ahead and pull out a bright, fluorescent yellow highlighter and mark the word. It's a key indicator of what's to come.

The science part is also valid but it creates too many unnecessary debates and this introductory book is about clarity, simplification, and structure.

Written in the spirit of 18th-century political economist and philosopher, Adam Smith, who is dubbed the "Father of Modern Economics," the aim is to present the first comprehensive text on a field of study that is alive and bubbling, and extremely relevant in mainstream society.

Whether you acknowledge it or not, there is an ever-growing strip club culture. All you have to do is utter these three words, "Make It Rain," and watch the hands around you start flicking away. And although the strip club industry is evolving and expanding into new territories, the economy is still going strong like the relationship between a **Regular** (patron) and a **Favorite** (stripper). But as a discipline, it is undisclosed, unaccredited and shunned in the halls of academia.

It's not hard to understand why.

Just use your imagination.

After a 30-minute VIP with two strippers named Kenzie and Monique, it wouldn't take long for a conservative economist to reevaluate the concept of fieldwork. The strip club experience is not an abstract science—it's a *social* science. It takes engagement, investment and one's willingness to play the strip club game (theory).

So, with the primary focus on the social dynamic, economics is defined as:

The study of behavior and choice in a social environment governed by a determining factor called scarcity.

Scarcity deals with the fact that individuals have unlimited wants and desires, but resources (goods & services) themselves are limited and finite.

Despite your inner child, and contrary to popular belief—you can't always get what you want. And that's before you even deal with the phrase, "Be careful what you ask for."

Interpretation: those that make the **rational** decision to enter a strip club looking to quench their thirst will not always find that unlimited source of satisfaction.

That's the mystique of the strip club and why it's called the jungle.

Pull back the curtain, and right there shrouded in darkness and sexuality is a hard lesson in opportunity cost. Which leads us to a new branch of economics appropriately called **Strip Club Economics**. The term is used loosely on social media, mainly as a hashtag (#StripClubEconomics). It's thrown around with no definition and backing—until now.

Strip Club Economics is defined as:

The study of behavior and choice in a strip club environment fueled by money and governed by two determining factors: thirst and scarcity.

Some outsiders and anti-strip club enthusiasts may consider Strip Club Economics a dismal science—full of wasted resources and a plaguing case of blue balls—but that's far from the truth. With a healthy attitude and a clear agenda, the strip club can be one of the best sources of entertainment.

But before you can learn more about the curriculum, you first have to answer the 3 essential questions that are at the root of Strip Club Economics 101.

What strip club should I enter?
How should I best spend my time and money?
What specific goods & services should receive the majority of my resources?

A **Strip Club Economist** can answer these 3 questions with rationale and critical thought.

ECONOMIST NOTE

Strip Club Economics is a distinct discipline that is undisclosed and unaccredited in the halls of higher education. You know why! The strip club is a topic too fraught with pitfalls for most economists to discuss.

LAW

2

THIRST AND SCARCITY

Our necessities are few but our wants are endless.

—Fortune Cookie

Strip club economics is the study of behavior and choice in a strip club environment fueled by money and governed by two determining factors: **thirst and scarcity**. Those two words alone, kick-start the economic engine that runs the multibillion-dollar strip club industry.

As coined in *The 21 Laws of Being an Exotic Dancer*, thirst is appropriately defined as:

The Hasty Instinctual Reaction to Sexual Tantalization

The
Hasty
Instinctual
Reaction to
Sexual
Tantalization

At the foundation of strip club economics, **thirst** represents the insatiable appetite and unlimited desire for T and A. It's derived from the animalistic urge to sexually activate all five senses (sight, hearing, smell, touch, and taste). In action, it's the following:

The eagerness to see it up close.
The relaxation from hearing a seductive voice.
The yearning to touch, caress, and feel the goosebumps on a curvy body.
The awakening from smelling the essence of pure sexuality.
And lastly, the lustful passion to taste the forbidden fruit.

And the one thing about **thirst** is that it's never fully quenched. At best, it's only temporally satisfied with a 3-minute lap dance or better yet, a 30-minute VIP. But the **thirst** and lust for more; the craving to drink from the bottomless cup of wants and desires is never satisfied. The **thirst** is ever-present, overpowering, and it often overlooks real-life limitations and consequences. Especially when you take those urges and add in the mental aspect—the *imagination.* Nothing can compete with a vivid and wild imagination.

An 18-year-old virgin can enter a strip club and imagine not only getting a lap dance from every single stripper in the room, but he's also fantasizing about his first orgy and guess who the main attraction is?

It's all in his head; a figment of his **thirsty** imagination.

Scarcity

But in reality, once you step foot into the strip club, and succumb to its capitalistic nature, it doesn't matter how thirsty you are, and how sexually-free and wild your imagination is. You are at the mercy of the strip club environment. And it's impossible to quench your thirst and have a lap dance with every single stripper in the room—most of all, at the same time.

In truth, that mind-blowing orgy comes at a hefty price—you gotta pay to play.

Scarcity *deals with the fact that although patrons have unlimited thirst for T and A, they also have a limited amount of resources, and a finite number of strippers that can (temporarily) quench that thirst and provide the ultimate Strip Club Fantasy.*

And there are no guarantees in the strip club game (theory). You have to roll the dice and hope you don't crap out. There are wins, but more often than not—losses.

A **Strip Club Economist** knows that you have to control your thirst, choose wisely, and always act in your own self-interest.

ECONOMIST NOTE

The concept of thirst and scarcity govern the strip club industry like survival and reproduction govern the jungle. There at the root of the strip club industry.

LAW 3

MICRO (G-STRING) ECONOMICS VS. MACRO (INDUSTRY) ECONOMICS

Economics is really politics in disguise.

—Hazel Henderson

Strip club economics is divided into two major categories: Micro (G-string) economics and Macro (industry) economics. Both interlocking categories allow the patron to discuss various strip club topics and concepts with clarification and political savvy. Most strip club conversations are flooded with endless opinions, assumptions and slanted judgments. Strip clubs are serious business and they deserve serious discourse.

MICRO (G-STRING) ECONOMICS 2-4-1

Micro (G-string) economics deals with the 'small picture'—hence, the prefix *micro-* and the insertion of the word G-string.

Who doesn't like a micro G-string?

The G-string symbolizes the one-on-one interaction between the stripper and the individual consumer: the patron. It's a focus on their behavior and decision making within the complexities of the strip club and outside the strip club.

For example, if you're discussing the following:

- The intimate dealings between a patron and a stripper in a VIP booth.
- The most popular strip club in town has changed their cover charge and Happy Hour prices.
- Tasty Thursdays is now the best day to go to ________ and blow a check.
- A mega-strip club called _______ is opening up at the beginning of next month.
- The overall talent level at _________ has severely dropped and it's time to visit their rival.

- Your Favorite (stripper) has relocated to a new strip club and changed her phone number.

You are engaging in the details and intricacies of Micro (G-string) economics 2-4-1.

MACRO (INDUSTRY) ECONOMICS

Macro (industry) economics deals with the 'big picture'—hence, the prefix *macro-* and the insertion of the word industry. It's a focus on the overall business aspect of the industry as a whole. It takes a more aggregate view on strip club economics, one that goes beyond the one-on-one interaction between the stripper and the patron.

For example, if you're discussing the following:

- What city has the best strip clubs? Las Vegas or Atlanta?
- ________ is by far the best strip club in the nation!
- What role does social media play in the marketing of strip clubs and their goods & services?
- Is the strip club becoming too mainstream?
- Will the job requirements of the strip

club waitress continue to evolve?

Furthermore, Macro (industry) economics also deals with forecasts and the authoritative role of local governments, city officials, and VICE.

- Will lap dances lose their appeal and become a thing of the past?
- Why is California conservative, compared to cities like Houston and New Orleans?
- Is minimum wage a good thing for strippers and how does it change the hustle?
- In 2031, will strip clubs even be a thing?

You are covering topics about the 'big picture' of Macro (industry) economics.

ECONOMIST NOTE

Knowing the difference between Micro (G-string) economics and Macro (industry) economics is essential when discussing and analyzing the strip club industry and its multiple variables.

LAW
4

THE CLASSICAL THEORY

In economic theory the conclusions are sometimes less interesting than the route by which they are reached.

—Piero Sraffa

In strip club economics, there are three main economic theories (Law 4-6) that fundamentally guide patron behavior and agenda.

Each theory contains its own set of real-world actions and beliefs that uniquely support (positively or negatively) the modern-day strip club industry and its function within adult entertainment. By endorsing a particular theory, the patron is casting their vote for the direction of the industry and its sustainability. They are also influencing and molding an ever-growing strip club culture.

The strip club economist knows exactly what theory is more advantageous to their bottom line and most effective to fostering the relationship between supply and demand—the stripper and the patron.

THE CLASSICAL THEORY

This introductory book is deeply rooted in the classical theory. The principle behind the classical theory is that the sole purpose to visit a strip club is to interact (mentality, physically and financially) with the one and only, main attraction: the stripper. Ideally, your Favorite (stripper). Everything else is secondary and a convenient distraction.

The word 'classical' relates to the tried-and-true business model of an old-school strip club—it's all about T and A.

Period.

It's not rocket science.

The classical strip club doesn't reinvent the wheel. The establishment knows that the only pure motivation is climbing to the top of the pyramid (see Fig. 1).

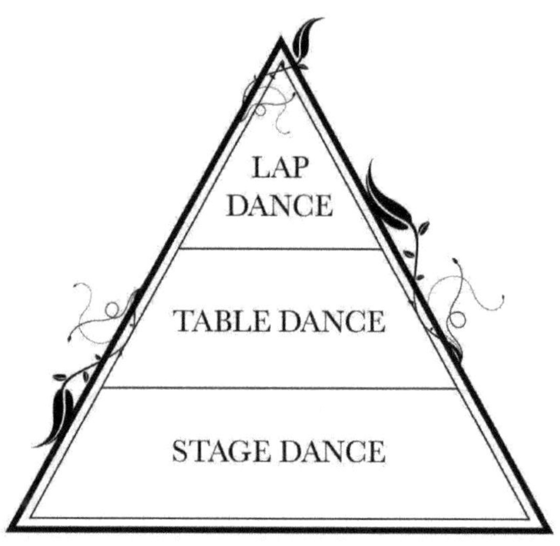

Fig. 1. Patron's Hierarchy of Needs.
From *The 21 Laws of Surviving a Gentlemen's Club* (p. 4), 2017, Varsity Club Publishing.

A **rational** patron doesn't go to the strip club to be a groupie for some celebrity or socialite hosting. They also don't go to the strip club for the primary reason to eat $2 buffalo wings and guzzle a pitcher of beer and then proceed to ignore the strippers on stage.

The signature item on the menu is and always will be the stripper. She provides all the essential nutrients for the patron's thirst and appetite for a strip club fantasy.

As long as strip clubs promote the main attraction and take care of their strippers, everything else falls into place—the true meaning of the term **laissez-faire**. In strip club economics, the French term **laissez-faire** means to:

Let go, and the strip club game (theory) will take care of itself.

When the stripper is the primary source of entertainment, supply and demand are guaranteed to meet at an equilibrium. Bangs go off like fireworks on the Fourth of July, and the stripper secures her bag of money. And for the grand finale, the patron's thirst is temporarily quenched.

Everyone is satisfied.

Again, **laissez-faire** is the key.

1. The free market is self-regulating.
2. Self-interest is the catalyst.
3. There's no bells and whistles needed.
4. No government intervention required.

That's the **invisible hand** at work, magically guiding the strip club game (theory) along, helping supply and demand connect with efficiency.

A strip club is called a strip club for a reason. As long as strip clubs keep the focus on the stripper, the money will keep coming in and the lights will stay on forever.

ECONOMIST NOTE

The classical theory is 'classical' for a reason. It focuses on the core relationship that stimulates the entire strip club industry: the one between the stripper and the patron. Everything else comes in a distant second.

LAW
5

THE RAPPER THEORY

I'm the top rapper in the world.

—Future

The principle behind the rapper theory is that the naturally flamboyant, self-absorbed rapper has strongly influenced patron behavior and indirectly modified strip club etiquette. For better or worse, they have created a legion of patrons who emulate their style and swagger.

Because of hip-hop and its competitive nature, it's incumbent upon the rags to riches rapper to desire the throne and aspire to be crowned the *best rapper alive.* Or at least, strive to be the hottest rapper in the game.

This ambition comes with the territory.

The rapper inherently wants all the shine, and occasionally all the smoke.

It's precisely that type of kinglike swag and brash attitude that carries over into the VIP of every strip club in America. The rapper believes that they are the King of the strip club and the spotlight is on them. As a result, the rapper takes a *more active* role in making the strip club a 'movie' experience (the rap video is passé).

Unlike the classical theory, when the rapper enters the strip club, they are the main attraction, the lead actor and the box office draw.

They posses the Star Power.

Everyone knows that the rapper would never be an extra in a strip club movie.

Playing the background is not an option.

This theory is far from a knock on rappers and hip-hop per se. The rapper's position is understandable and quite customary, especially given the climate in hip-hop and its strong business ties to strip clubs and their DJs. For most rappers, the strip club is a viable source of income and status. When you consider the fact that a lot of rappers create a buzz by breaking their songs at strip clubs, it's a smart business move.

And let's be honest, rappers are solely responsible for the popularity of the "Make It Rain" movement that's been going strong ever since Fat Joe and Lil Wayne released their smash hit in 2006.

Truth be told if it weren't for rain showers, thunderstorms, and bottles poppin', a lot of strip clubs wouldn't be able to stay in business.

Hate it or love it, rappers are a mainstay in the strip club scene.

But the driving factor behind this economic theory is the powerful *influence* that rappers have on impressionable patrons who mimic their behavior and attitude towards strippers and the strip club environment.

Consequently, a new generation of patrons are entering the establishment with with the goal of being the King of the strip club and competing with the stripper for top billing. This type of patron wants the attention and the spotlight that is supposed to be reserved for the dancer on stage.

And they're willing to achieve that goal by any means necessary.

They have no desire in a strip club fantasy. The lap dance is a distraction and a hindrance. The concept of supply and demand, means they supply the blessing and the stripper demands their royal presence. The only equilibrium achieved is the balance needed to hold the money phone close to the ear.

Is this a problem?

Not exactly.

For many, filling the expensive shoes of the 'rapper' and becoming the focal point of the night is the best way to enjoy the strip club, or create the ultimate strip club experience.

It's all about moviemaking.

And in various urban strip clubs in leading cities like Atlanta, Los Angeles and Houston not only encourage and support the rapper theory, but they feel strongly that the classical theory is outdated, boring and too traditional for the evolving times.

The future is now.

But proponents of the classical theory have three essential questions for advocates of the rapper theory and its unforeseen consequences.

Who drives the strip club economy, the rapper or the stripper?
Can you have too many Kings and not enough Merchants?
Is the rapper the right person to model strip club etiquette?

Therein lies the differences in strip club ideology, philosophy, and theory.

ECONOMIST NOTE

The rapper theory is a direct reflection of the influential role that rappers play in modern-day strip club culture. The questions are, what are they influencing and is it worth imitating?

LAW
6

THE NEOCLASSICAL THEORY

Neoclassical economics insists that advertising cannot force consumers to buy anything they don't already want to buy.

—Christopher Lasch

The neoclassical theory is a newly evolving theory based on the stipulation that the only way modern-day strip clubs can compete in an oversaturated market is to take a multi-purpose, all-encompassing, buffet-style entertainment approach to an otherwise classical business model.

Most strip clubs today are a mix between a trendy hip-hop nightclub, a traditional sports bar, and a popular restaurant chain. It's a free-for-all, with a mega menu of food and activities. They welcome every type of patron with open pockets, even the wallflowers, outsiders and anti-strip club enthusiasts. As long as they spend money on alternative goods & services, it doesn't matter who the main attraction is. It's all about the club's bottom line.

In this neoclassical strip club, the stripper is a role player, an extra in the overall strip club experience. She's not the headliner. Everything at this club has equal billing:

Alcohol = Tacos = Pizza = Burger and Fries = Buffalo Wings = Chicken Tenders = T-Bone Steak = Caesar Salad = Hookah = Flat-Screen Television

=

Pool Table = Strip Club DJ = Bartender = Waitress

=

Stripper

They're all on the same level. The strip club doesn't have a traditional hierarchy. There is no stripper standing at the top of the pyramid (Patron's Hierarchy of Needs) overlooking the environment and confidently knowing that she is the main attraction—the Star of the Show. At its core, the neoclassical strip club is more like a Dave & Buster's or a Buffalo Wild Wings with the addition of strippers. You can 'Make It Rain' or make it a point to sit, bypass the stripper, and watch the ballgame over a plate of hot wings and a pitcher of beer.

THE THREE CENTRAL ASSUMPTIONS IN NEOCLASSICAL THEORY

- **Patrons**: They act independently and no longer have any brand loyalty to strippers. They are too vain and self-centered to play the strip club game (theory).
- **Discretion and Privacy**: They are a thing of the past. It's all about the party, and showing everyone on social media that you party like a rock star.
- **Lap Dances**: The once coveted lap dance has lost its appeal. The invisible hand is no longer instrumental in guiding patrons into the VIP booth. It's now vital to create alternative types of entertainment to preoccupy the patron's attention.

As the industry evolves and competition stiffens, more club owners will continue to take the neoclassical approach and look into new ways of reinventing the wheel. Neoclassical patrons will gladly spread out their resources on various menu items, instead of concentrating their time and money on the once perceived main attraction: the stripper.

Times have changed, so strip clubs should change as well, correct? Proponents of the classical theory strongly disagree.

The conversation continues... And time will tell what theory proves to be at the forefront of the strip club industry.

ECONOMIST NOTE

The neoclassical theory is a timely response to the intense competition between modern-day strip clubs to attract a new type of strip club patron. This theory is gaining ground and popularity, but to what detriment?

LAW
7

WHAT'S THE INCENTIVE?

Most of economics can be summarized in four words: "People respond to incentives." The rest is commentary.

—Steven Landsburg

What strip club should I enter? Before any patron can obey their thirst and answer that pivotal question, they must first know what a strip club offers. Why go to a strip club? What can you expect?

What exactly is it that gives a person case of FOMO (Fear of missing out)?

Of course, one can bypass the strip club and

spend their time doing the following activities:

- Do absolutely nothing.
- Netflix & Chill …or just Netflix.
- Be a couch potato and binge watch your favorite show on HBO.
- Play a video game and compete against players online.
- Open up your black-book and text an old friend “Hey stranger.” Don’t forget the emoji.
- Work on your Fantasy Football Team and overdose on NFL highlights.
- Listen to an audiobook, while you workout.
- Lose yourself on YouTube until you fall dead asleep.
- Stay at home and read that book that’s been stuck on chapter 1.
- Head across the border to Tijuana and hook up with a Selena Gomez lookalike.
- Have a guys’ night out and catch up on old times.
- Buy credits and say hello to your favorite cam girl or subscribe to a sex worker’s premium accounts (OnlyFans, Snapchat, SubscribePlace, etc.) and binge out.

- Go on a swiping spree and see if you can catch a fish on a dating app.
- Post up at a nightclub and shoot your shot, James Harden style.
- Hit a bar and open up a tab.
- Take it back to the 70s and grab a nudie magazine and hide out in the bathroom.
- Visit your local mega movie theatre and watch a blockbuster movie.
- Go on a date and try to work your magic.
- Log onto Pornhub and search for the perfect, raunchy porn scene to relieve your stress.
- Send a bunch of thirsty DMs to your favorite Instagram models and hope for a response.
- Strike up conversations with old flames on Facebook and try to rekindle the fire.
- Hire an escort and get a real Girlfriend Experience.
- Try a new sex position with your newly acquired sex doll girlfriend, Ginger.
- Save your resources and watch your Favorite (stripper) twerk on Instagram.

As you can see, there are tons of entertainment options that you can explore. So, why go to a strip club? What's the incentive? The incentive is that a stripper provides a goods & service called a **Strip Club Fantasy**. Outsiders and critics will never understand its benefits. But strip club economists and enthusiasts know that it's an entertainment bundle like no other. It's a grab bag full of sexuality, mystery and intrigue. The bundle is packed with:

THIRST,
FUN, LUST,
T AND A, FEMININITY,
EYE CANDY, PARTY ANIMALS,
HEDONISM, DANGEROUS LIAISONS,
FLIRTATION, SEXUAL ENERGY,
BEAUTIFUL LIES, THERAPY SESSIONS,
ESCAPISM,
FREAKINESS, GIRLFRIEND EXPERIENCES,
TANTALIZATION,
EXTRACURRICULAR ACTIVITY,
STRIPPER GAMESMANSHIP, HOSPITALITY,
CUSTOMER SERVICE,
INSTANT GRATIFICATION, FREE SPIRITS,
SECRETS, MIND GAMES, CARNALITY,
SEDUCTION,
RATCHETNESS, DISCRETION,
COMPANIONSHIP,
EXOTIC DANCING, EXOTICISM, SEX TALK,
EGO STROKING, ROLE PLAY, TWERKING,
MIND FUCKING, PUSSY POWER,
POLE DANCING, STAGE SHOWS,
INTIMACY, EROTICISM,
AND
HIGH-MILEAGE
LAP DANCES

Altogether, the stripper serves up a spicy concoction, mixed with entertainment and human nature. And you can only get it at a strip club. That's the incentive.

ECONOMIST NOTE

Knowing the power of incentives and the role they play in Strip Club Economics is vital to studying a patron's behavior and choice.

LAW 8

THERE'S NO SUCH THING AS A FREE TOUCH

The most basic law of economics, namely that one cannot get something for nothing.

—Sir Henry Roy Forbes Harrod

There's a popular phrase that resonates with all economists and hard working citizens that keep their nose to the grindstone.

"There's No Such Thing As A Free Lunch" (TNSTAAFL)

The phrase refers to the idea that absolutely

nothing in this world is free—you can't get something for nothing. It's used as a stark reminder that one should get off their lazy tail and get to work. The word *free* is often used loosely and deceptively. Everything has a cost involved. It can be financially, mentality, physically, and hell, even spiritually.

In economics, the idea of free is explored in a concept called opportunity cost, further discussed in Law 10.

However, in Strip Club Economics, the phrase TNSTAAFL is twerked a little bit. It goes as follows:

"There's No Such Thing As A Free Touch" (TNSTAAFT)

The addition of **touch** symbolizes the interaction between a stripper and a patron, and the saying as a whole represents the capitalistic environment.

On a Micro (G-String) economic level, a stripper will be the first one to tell you that 'nothing is free.' Tipping is expected and please don't come to the strip club empty-handed.

The ATM is at the back.

But TNSTAAFT goes beyond the stereotypical, money hungry stripper that wants to express her demands and stipulations—and most often her frustrations about freeloaders. There is a deeper economic meaning behind her sentiments.

Not only is being a stripper a job, but it's one that takes a significant amount of money to be successful.

Presentation matters! And that presentation comes with a cost.

Nothing is free.

Your Favorite (stripper) didn't hop out of bed, head straight to work, and hit the stage. It took time for her to sit in the dressing room and get dolled up with the goal of quenching your thirst.

Here's a glimpse of the hidden cost that's hidden behind a sexy smile and the acceptance of a $1 tip.

Makeup	**$200.00**
Perfume/Lotion	**$40.00**
Outfit	**$60.00**
Stripper Heels	**$70.00**
Hair	**$175.00**
Pedi/Mani	**$100.00**
Gas	**$20.00**
House Fee	**$75.00**
Total	**$740.00**

And some strippers will gladly inform you that this is on the low-end side of things. Not listed are the costs of plastic surgery and other enhancements. You get the point.

The **Strip Club Economist** knows that to enter

the strip club to be a spectator and spend *zero money* is not only **irrational**, but it violates the very economic nature of an environment that is fueled by money.

ECONOMIST NOTE

In a strip club, everything comes at a cost. The only thing that's free is the directions to the closest ATM.

LAW 9

SUPPLY AND DEMAND

Supply always comes on the heels of demand.

—Robert Collier

The supply and demand curve has long been an effective tool that allows the average person to understand and visualize a free-market at work. It takes an extremely dynamic concept (price determination) and simplifies it to highlight the magnetic relationship between supply and demand; one that results in a price and a quantity of a goods & service being sold.

When all factors remain equal, an equilibrium is achieved.

And in Strip Club Economics—specifically in classical theory, when supply meets demand, the fireworks from a lap dance go off with a Bang, and what happens in the dark, stays in the dark.

Strip club economists use the supply and demand curve as a model to analyze the core relationship that makes the strip club economy flourish—the Stripper and the Patron.

THE STRIP CLUB SUPPLY AND DEMAND CURVE

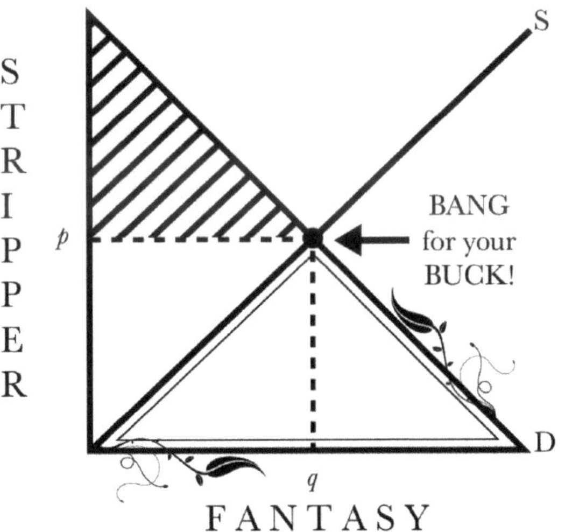

Fig. 1. The Strip Club Supply and Demand Curve

SUPPLY

The Stripper supplies the Strip Club Fantasy for a price. The main feature of that Strip Club Fantasy is the coveted lap dance. The properties of Supply are represented by an upward-sloping curve (S): if the price increases, the quantity of the Strip Club Fantasy increases in a variety of sexy ways, in effect increasing the Stripper's money bag.

DEMAND

The Patron's thirst creates a demand for the Strip Club Fantasy and the coveted lap dance is the primary service that takes care of the Patron's Hierarchy of Needs—all five senses are activated. The properties of Demand are represented by a downward-sloping curve (D): if the price increases to a ridiculous amount and money is limited, the quantity demanded of the Strip Club Fantasy decreases.

PRICE (*p*)

The (*p*) is the price of the Strip Club Fantasy and the coveted lap dance. The price varies and shifts per goods & service (ex. $20 per song, $40 per song, $150 for 15 Minutes, $250 for 30 minutes), the type of establishment (topless, bikini bar, fully-nude, etc.) and location (city and state).

QUANTITY (*q*)

The (*q*) is the quantity of the Strip Club Fantasy. The quantity varies in degrees, doses, intensities, temperatures, mileage, chemistry, intimacy, and extracurricular activity.

EQUILIBRIUM

The equilibrium is the point where Supply and Demand meet. Both parties reach an even or reasonable exchange; a balanced, lustful, capitalistic trade-off between the Stripper and the Patron.

As the Patron climbs the pyramid (Patron's Hierarchy of Needs), the equilibrium is reached at the top of the pyramid with a lap dance. (Look closely at Fig. 1, the pyramid is present). And in classical theory, that's where the patron feels they got the most Bang for their Buck. The patron's thirst was quenched, albeit temporarily.

Those with sensitive ears will quickly question, "What is the Bang?" For some, it will immediately conjure up dirty thoughts and rude behavior. But the BANG in the phrase 'Bang for your Buck' is the immediate:

Benefit
Acquired
Not including
Gratuity

Meaning, if you spend $20 on a lap dance or spend $100 on a VIP when you exit that booth, you leave with the genuine feeling that you got your money's worth. And that's before you make the noble decision to add a tip or anything else that would be considered gratuity. Giving a tip would be like putting extra icing on a cake that has already satisfied your sweet tooth. Now that's a worthwhile purchase.

ECONOMIST NOTE

The dynamics of supply and demand are at the heart of the relationship between a stripper and a patron. And without that connection, the strip club economy would be weak and unsustainable.

LAW 10

THE OPPORTUNITY COST AND THE SUNK COST OF PLAYING THE STRIP CLUB GAME (THEORY)

Economics is a choice between alternatives all the time. Those are the trade-offs.

—Paul Samuelson

Inside the strip club, the following phrase applies to every patron willing to roll the dice and play the strip club game (theory):

You Gotta Pay The Cost, To Be The Boss

Nothing is free. But what exactly is the cost?

Well, in actuality, there are two main costs at play.

Opportunity cost and **sunk cost**.

First, let's deal with opportunity cost.

The first stage of opportunity cost is making the **rational** decision to enter a strip club over alternative choices of entertainment (examples in Law 7).

The second stage of opportunity cost deals with the benefits and the losses (time and money) that come with trying to choose the right stripper for your Strip Club Fantasy—essentially, attempting to answer the classic question, "Who will provide the most Bang for your Buck?"

You must choose wisely, and take advantage of your limited opportunities.

On the opposite end of the word, Bang is the word Sunk.

When you choose the *wrong* stripper and completely miss the Bang in your Buck, the money spent is a sunk cost. A sunk cost is not just a typical loss of money—losing money is bound to happen in a strip club. But it's the money spent that you specifically regret because you painfully made a terrible investment. You know that you can't get a penny back and that money has sunken into the ocean of disappointment.

And that ocean is overflowing with boatloads of money.

Tons of money.

There's a reason why it's called **the strip club game (theory).** There are wins, but more often than not—losses.

The Strip Club Game (Theory) *is the observation and study of how patrons and strippers behave and interact strategically in a strip club environment fueled by money and influenced by self-interest, motives, and agendas. Each participant is playing to win advantage and position.*

The most common game that exemplifies the game within the strip club game (theory) is the Patron's Dilemma.

THE PATRON'S DILEMMA

SCENARIO 1

The roll call is full of sexy strippers that are ready to give you an unforgettable Strip Club Fantasy, topped off with a mind-blowing lap dance.

1. SAPPHIRE
2. PEACHES 3. MIA 4. DEVINE
5. STACEY 6. CHLOE 7. SUMMER
8. AUSTIN 9. BELLA
10 .CANDY 11. GINA 12. ANASTASIA
13. AMBER 14. SAHARA 15. RUBY 16. MIAMI
17. COCO
18. MARY JANE 19. FINESSE
20. ZOEY
21. DIAMOND

On the surface, choosing the right stripper seems easy. Just obey your thirst and spot your favorite eye candy. But in reality, the strip club game (theory) is never that easy.

Patron A walks into a strip club with $300 to spend and only 2 hours to accomplish that goal. The clock is already ticking and given the club's prices ($20 per song, $40 per song, $150 for 15 minutes, $250 for 30 minutes), his $300 can get swallowed up pretty quickly. And it doesn't help that he's itching for a steamy VIP, which costs $250 for 30 minutes of mystery and intrigue.

Within the first hour, three different strippers (**Amber**, **Coco**, and **Candy**) approach, and initiate a small conversation. They all end the meet and greet with the same question. "Would you like a lap dance?"

	Dilemma
Amber	**Drop-dead gorgeous, model-type but her conversation was a bit scripted.**
Coco	**Sweetheart, girl-next-door type with a bubbly personality and the conversation was entertaining.**
Candy	**Sexy, assertive, straight to the point and she kept the conversation fun and naughty.**

Looks-wise, the patron can't stop staring at **Amber**, whose body is absolutely stunning. But inside, he feels more at ease with **Coco** and **Candy**. They both come off as more genuine and appreciative of the moment. But his vivid imagination has taken over and he proceeds to jump into the deep end and get a VIP with **Amber**.

He's putting his chips all in.

Well, at least $250.

They head upstairs and disappear into the dark. Forty-five minutes later, he returns with a headache and an unpleasant frown. His head is hurting from **Amber's** random chatter about her ex-husband being a jerk and her plans on retiring from the strip club game (theory) and opening up a marijuana dispensary. He wanted some intimacy, but he ended up feeling like an overworked psychiatrist.

He slumps down in an open seat and thinks about the $250 (<u>sunk cost</u>) that just sunk into the ocean of disappointment. While moping and checking the time, a pleasant surprise takes a seat right next to him and gives a welcoming smile. It's **Coco**, and they immediately pick up where they left off. She's saying all the right things and he's thinking about getting 2 lap dances at $20 per song, leaving him with $10 and a great excuse to leave.

So, he decides to go out with a Bang.

They both walk over to a neighboring booth and take a seat. Two songs later, he's smiling and thirsting for more. To his surprise, he got his money's worth. **Coco** not only had the Midas touch, but her levels of seduction were unexpected. More importantly, he learned a hard lesson about opportunity cost. He rolled the dice on **Amber** and it cost him $250.

FORMULA FOR CALCULATING OPPORTUNITY COST

Opportunity cost = the stripper you feel you should have chosen and the great time you missed out on - the reality that you chose the wrong stripper and the sunk cost blown on a forgettable experience.

Patron A is wishing he had that $250 to spend on a VIP with **Coco**. Best believe, on his next visit, he will play the strip club game (theory) differently and not make the same mistake on **Amber**.

Opportunity cost, sunk cost and the complexities of the strip club game (theory) are the real reasons why critics and anti-strip club enthusiasts consider the strip club a foolish, self-defeating type of entertainment. They know that things can spiral out of control and the results of the strip club game (theory) can be costly to one's psyche and bank account.

ECONOMIST NOTE

In the strip club game (theory), you have to "pay the cost to be the boss." And the opportunity cost and the sunk cost is what's really at stake.

LAW
11

COST AND BENEFIT

It's a risk-reward, cost-benefit analysis, when you think about it. Sometimes it bites him, sometimes he comes out on the winning end of things.

—Tim Ryan

A **rational** patron knows the **incentives** of going to a strip club and what to expect. They are confident and secure with their decision to enter the strip club. They are also familiar with both stages of **opportunity cost**, and they understand the risks of rolling the dice and possibly taking a loss (sunk cost). It's all part of the strip club game (theory). But even with their conviction, they can still find themselves defending their thirst for strip clubs and their willingness to partake in a type of entertainment that is self-defeating and financially draining.

Not many can relate.

What those on the outside looking in don't consider is the real-life costs and benefits of going to the strip club to interact with strippers versus going out in the real-world and interacting with citizens. Indeed, there are immediate and long-lasting trade-offs.

Table 1. COST-BENEFIT ANALYSIS

Listed below is a realistic cost-benefit analysis that highlights the potential costs and benefits that come with the decision to enter a strip club and indulge in a strip club fantasy.

	Cost
	• **Money (an arm and a leg)** • **Energy** • **Time** • **Sanity (mind games)** • **Privacy (public place)** • **Opportunity Cost** • **Health (food & alcohol)** • **A Pair of Jeans (glitter stains)** • **Case of Blue Balls**

	Benefit
	• **Saves You Money (versus dating)** • **Saves You Time (cut to the chase)** • **Saves You Energy (no chasing)** • **No Child Support Payments due from a Previous Lap Dance** • **No STD from a Lap Dance (in majority cases)** • **Saves You Unwanted Attachment** • **Safe Entertainment (legal)** • **No Sexual Harassment Allegations** • **No Unplanned Pregnancy from a Lap Dance** • **Private Fun (in the dark)** • **Diversity of Women** • **Freedom to Express Your Sexuality**

Critics and outsiders rarely mention the benefits of entering a strip club, but a **Strip Club Economist** discusses the pros and cons with rationale and practicality.

ECONOMIST NOTE

The real-life costs and benefits of entering a strip club are rarely discussed with depth and seriousness. When you consider some of the benefits, going to a strip club doesn't sound so bad after all.

LAW 12

VALUE YOUR TWO MAIN RESOURCES: TIME AND MONEY

Many people take no care of their money till they come nearly to the end of it, and others do just the same with their time.

—Johann Wolfgang von Goethe

One of the essential questions in strip club economics is *how should I best spend my time and money?*

A question that exemplifies the broad study of behavior and choice. If you ask 100 patrons, you'll get 100 different answers.

The **Strip Club Economist** knows that before you approach that question with rationale and prudence, you must first *value* the two main resources pinpointed in that core question: **time** and **money**.

Fundamentally, what else do you have in a strip club?

TIME

Time is of the essence and unless you plan on bringing a sleeping bag and camping out in your favorite strip club in Las Vegas (open 24 hrs), the majority of the time you will have to deal with a time constraint. Regardless if you visit on a Day-shift or a Night-shift, you must take advantage of your precious time and make it worth the visit. Seize the moment. Thoroughly experience the strip club and move with purpose. No one in their right mind goes to the strip club to waste time. As soon as you enter the door, the proverbial clock is ticking and you don't have all day trying to find the right stripper to get the most Bang for your Buck.

It's best to be timely and opportunistic.

The **rational** patron values their time.

If not, why even enter a strip club? You can spend your valuable time elsewhere.

MONEY

It's no secret that money fuels the strip club. And the more you have, the more you can play the strip club game (theory). But you must be completely honest with yourself. Put your pride to the side, and live in reality.

How much money are you working with?
What are you willing to spend?
Do you have the discipline to stick to that amount?

As much as you want to be a member of The Money Team (TMT)—you gotta keep it 100. Most patrons are part of The Budget Team (TBT). And that's okay.

It's your bank account.

Money is a resource that should not be given out as charity. Are you really trying to throw a scholarship?

Even so, you want to make sure you get a good return on your investment (ROI). Money doesn't grow on trees, and once you throw it, you can't get it back. There are no refunds in the strip club.

The strip club game (theory) is unforgiving.

You must be calculated and economical, but keep in mind, that's not an excuse to be cheap and stingy. It means you value a resource that 'makes the world go around' and you understand its power.

ECONOMIST NOTE

Time and money are precious resources that need to be valued and taken seriously. At the end of the day, that's all you have in a strip club.

LAW
13

INVEST IN THE BARE MARKET

Markets work well with goods that economists call private.

—Eric Maskin

What makes a strip cub a strip club?

The **rational** patron knows exactly why they're entering a strip club and what market is the primary market that deserves the majority of their resources (time and money).

In today's modern strip club, there are several different markets at play. The neoclassical theory is on the rise and the way the strip club industry is evolving clubs will continue to expand on their menu of goods & services and create additional ways to attract a wider customer base and maximize profits at all costs. Regardless, if it redefines the definition of a classical strip club—one that centers around the main attraction: the stripper.

Some establishments are blurring lines so much that you can't even tell if they're a strip club or a nightclub or a sports bar. These neoclassical clubs are just one-stop shops for any and everything that can make a quick buck.

In classical theory, investing the majority of your resources in a non-bare market is **irrational** and counterproductive to getting the most Bang for your Buck. You must always know your true intentions for visiting a strip club and have an agenda that makes **rational** sense. Otherwise, why are going to a strip club, again?

Table 1. NON-BARE MARKET

Although the following markets do serve a purpose in creating an overall strip club experience and if you're a foodie, they can activate your five senses, Table 1 summarizes the fact that you can easily get these goods & services at alternative places (fast food chains, restaurants, diners, lounges, liquor stores, grocery stores, bars, etc.).

	Alternatives	No Alternatives
Alcoholic Beverage Market	X	
Taco Market	X	
Pizza Market	X	
Hookah Market	X	
Burger and Fries Market	X	
Hot Wings Market	X	
Chicken Tender Market	X	
T-Bone Steak Market	X	
Caesar Salad Market	X	
Lunch Buffet Market	X	

Table 2. ECONOMIC FORECAST 2019 - 2029

As competition intensifies, do not be surprised when you see an increase in strip clubs promoting the following markets:

	Alternatives	No Alternatives
Karaoke Market	X	
Comedy Show Market	X	
Domino Tournament Market	X	
Rap Show Market	X	
Special Guest DJ Market	X	
Celebrity Hosting Market	X	
Cage Fighting Market	X	

Table 3. BARE MARKET

Can you go to a fast food restaurant and get a fully nude lap dance? What about at a liquor store? How about a Hookah lounge? Surely, at a pizza parlor? Certainly at a diner? You get the point. There are no alternatives.

	Alternatives	No Alternatives
Lap Dance Market		X

Only at a strip club, can you get a sexy, high mileage lap dance from a stripper who's willing to bare it all (topless, naked, butt naked, birthday suit).

You can receive a private good in the privacy of a VIP booth.

Can you partake and indulge in those additional markets? Of course, but classically thinking, as long as you know that those items are secondary to the unique and rare service that only a stripper can provide—the strip club fantasy and the coveted lap dance—the true meaning of the bare market.

ECONOMIST NOTE

There is only one market that's worth the majority of your resources and that's the bare market, predominately available at the strip club.

LAW
14

EMBRACE THE MONOPOLY

Monopoly is the condition of every successful business.

—Peter Thiel

Strip club economics is a distinct discipline that takes traditional economic theories and concepts, and flips them upside down, twirls them on a pole and twerks them a bit. A great example is the case with monopolies. A **monopoly** refers to a corporation having a stranglehold of power over a given market. It's illegal and regulations are in place to prevent their existence.

But inside the strip club, there's a natural monopoly that must be embraced by all **rational** thinking patrons. It's the key factor that defines a strip club. It's not only legal, but it's a service that has zero alternatives and no substitutes. We are talking about the

STRIPPER'S MONOPOLY ON THE LAP DANCE MARKET

Through specialization, the stripper dominates the Lap Dance Market. She has the monopolistic power to control the supply of the strip club fantasy, and she is the single seller of its main feature: the coveted lap dance.

Table 1. LAP DANCE MARKET

	Lap Dance
Stripper	X
Waitress	
Bartender	

CHARACTERISTICS OF THE STRIPPER'S MONOPOLY

- **Barriers to Entry**: You must pay a house fee and have the necessary paperwork to be a stripper. There are clear job requirements. *Some clubs allow their waitresses and bartenders to* *invade the spaces reserved and assigned to strippers without proper certification. This is in direct violation to the Stripper's Monopoly on the Lap Dance Market.*

- **Single Seller**: She's the only one who can provide the coveted lap dance. Not the waitress and certainly not a twerking bartender.
- **Strip Club Fantasy maker**: The Stripper decides the type of fantasy that she wants to present to the patron.
- **Patron Discrimination**: At her discretion, the stripper can change the quantity of the strip club fantasy at any time.

PATRON'S HIERARCHY OF NEEDS

She's the only one that can activate all five senses and compel a patron to club up the pyramid with the passion and persistence of a thirsty mountain climber.

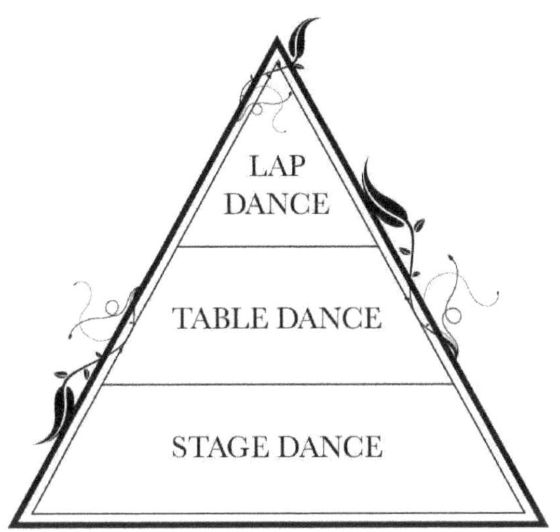

Fig. 1. Patron's Hierarchy of Needs.
From *The 21 Laws of Surviving a Gentlemen's Club* (p. 4), 2017, Varsity Club Publishing.

THE LAP DANCE INDEX OF MONOPOLY POWER

Strip club economists use the Lap Dance Index to measure and calculate a stripper's market power.

$$MP = (5S \times 3\Delta) + M\,(SCF \times T/P)$$

MP = Monopoly Power (Market Power)
5S = 5 Senses (sight, hearing, smell, touch, and fantasy of taste)
3 = 3 Levels of the pyramid on the Patron's Hierarchy of Needs
Δ = Patron's Hierarchy of Needs
SCF = Strip Club Fantasy (0-100 scale)
M = Mileage (0-10 scale)
T = Time (minutes of Lap Dance time)
P = Price (of the Lap Dance)

To calculate the value of the Lap Dance Index, **SCF** value, **Mileage** value, **Time**, and **Price** are needed.

Example: Patron A purchases a 15 minute VIP from **Gia** for the price of $100. After the VIP, he gives the SCF a value of 76 and the mileage value of the lap dance a 7.

$$\mathbf{MP = (5S \times 3\Delta) + 7\ (76 \times 15/100)}$$
$$15\Delta S + 7\ (1{,}140/100)$$
$$15\Delta S + 7 \times 11.4$$
$$15\Delta S + 79.8 = \mathbf{94.8\Delta S}$$

Not only did Patron A get his money's worth, but he also felt the market power of **Gia**, a stripper who's on her game.

ECONOMIST NOTE

The strip club economist knows exactly who has the monopolistic power to provide the most Bang for their Buck. It's called a 'strip' club for a reason. Embrace the monopoly and respect its power.

LAW
15

PURE COMPETITION

Competition is one of the most important drivers of innovation because you have to stay in the race. You have to think of something new, and if you don't, well, of course you should leave the market.

—Margrethe Vestager

Within the confines of the strip club and precisely on the main floor is one of the best examples of **pure competition**. On a Micro (G-string) economic level, the stripper has a welcoming monopoly on the lap dance market and she sits at the top of the hierarchy of strip club workers.

Stripper > Waitress > Bartender

But within the structure of **pure competition**, the stripper isn't the only one who can provide a steamy lap dance. She has to compete with a roll call full of strippers who are ready to compete and secure their bags. They too are working with limited time and a finite group of patrons willing to break the bank. And in a strip club, time is money.

CHARACTERISTICS OF PURE COMPETITION

- **Large Number**: There are always a larger number of strippers on the roll call selling a strip club fantasy.
- **Standardized product**: Strippers all provide the same goods & service: a strip club fantasy. Its main feature is the coveted lap dance.
- **Free entry and exit**: New strippers can enter the market and compete with veteran dancers on the main floor and on the main stage. They can also leave the stripper profession whenever they want.
- **Price taker**: The strip club sets the price on lap dances, not the stripper. (ex. $20 per song, $40 per song, $150 for 15 Minutes, $250 for 30 minutes).

The **rational** patron is aware of this market situation called **pure competition**. It's part of the strip club game (theory). It's the nature of the strip club environment. Competition is an integral part of a free-market with independent sellers offering the same product: a strip club fantasy.

As a result, a smart patron never falls for shaming tactics that deter competition and shy away from hustling and hard work.

- Guilt Trips
- Sob Stories
- Ultimatums
- Script Readings
- Tall Tales

The **Strip Club Economist** is always content with letting the chips fall where they may. They know that the **invisible hand** guides the market and the right stripper will eventually fall right into their lap.

ECONOMIST NOTE

Competition is an integral part of a free market at work, and on the main floor of a busy strip club, it doesn't get any purer.

LAW
16

LAW OF DIMINISHING RETURNS

The law of diminishing returns is something I really believe in.

—Thomas Keller

In Micro (G-string) economics, the law of diminishing returns is a simple yet powerful concept. It states that if a patron doesn't find a **Favorite** (stripper), they will always be subject to a stripper that provides a strip club fantasy that eventually diminishes in quality and quantity.

Let that sink in.

At first, you could be getting the most Bang for your Buck. But immediately, or over time, if she's not your **Favorite** (stripper) and you're not her **Regular** (patron), the Bang supplied will shift to new demand and gravitate to a higher source of income.

It's all part of the strip club game (theory).

A savvy dancer will always reserve the fireworks and the extracurricular activity for her **Regulars** (patrons).

In reality, strip club chemistry is scarce. Plus, a wise man once said, "You can't trust a big butt and a smile." The stripper you choose could possess the following qualities and characteristics:

- Crappy Attitude
- Bitterness
- Unprofessionalism
- Lack of Chemistry
- Amateurism
- Scamminess
- Unawareness of the Strip Club Game (Theory)
- Zero Personality
- Lack of Skills
- Having a Bad Day
- Bad script reading

The average stripper can mask these qualities and characteristics, but for only so long, especially if you're not <u>Regular material</u>. As a result, the patron is always confronted by the law of diminishing returns—a strip club fantasy that abruptly stops and turns into an open-handed slap of reality—another reason why many avoid strip clubs as a viable form of entertainment.

ECONOMIST NOTE

The law of diminishing returns is a stark reminder that you will never be highly favored if you haven't found a true Favorite (stripper).

LAW
17

LAW OF INCREASING RETURNS

In Micro (G-string) economics, the opposite of the law of diminishing returns is the law of increasing returns.

It's a concept that is central to strip club economics and its study of behavior and choice. In effect, the law highlights the core relationship between a **Regular** (patron) and a **Favorite** (stripper) and its power to sustain the business of an individual strip club and the entire strip club economy.

The law of increasing returns states that if a patron can find a true Favorite (stripper) to invest in and enjoy her many services, and become her Regular (patron)—<u>although the cost doesn't diminish</u>—the return on the investment increases on every visit. The value of the strip club fantasy only gets better and better over time until the Regular (patron) creates a self-induced ceiling and desires to take things outside the club and beyond the fantasy.

Otherwise, inside the strip club, the Favorite (stripper) is the best entertainment package that money can buy.

But what's the difference between a stripper and a Favorite (stripper)? Besides being highly sought after, a Favorite (stripper) is three times the average stripper.

THE POWER RULE OF THE FAVORITE (STRIPPER)

$$F(X) = X^{3}$$

F = Favorite **(X)** = (Stripper's Name)

X^{3} = Stripper to the 3rd Power

A true Favorite (stripper) is a stripper to the **3rd Power**. Whereas the average stripper can represent one column, the Favorite (stripper) represents all three. She is the following:

Feminine
Attractive
Vivacious
Open-minded
Ready
Intense
Tantalizing
Enticing

Fiery
Appreciative
Valuable
Optimistic
Reciprocal
Involved
Trustworthy
Enthusiastic

Freaky
Attentive
Vixenly
One-of-a-kind
Respectful
Intuitive
Therapeutic
Empowering

The Favorite (stripper) is the ultimate strip club fantasy. She is the one that enhances the strip club experience, elevating a typical encounter to an actual strip club relationship. She brings real value, reciprocity, and equilibrium to the supply and demand curve—Bang, Bang, Bang! She's worth every penny, receiving the majority of the Regular's resources, gifts, and tips.

For that reason, Favorite is a title that should not be given out without proper recognition and assessment.

PATRON'S CEILING

There is one surefire way to violate the law of increasing returns, and that is for the Regular (patron) to catch feelings and mandate a ceiling on the amount of money spent on their Favorite (stripper). Often thirst and lust take over, and the Regular (patron) believes that because they've spent a maximum amount of money inside the strip club, it's now obligatory to take their strip club relationship outside the strip club. They have emotionally and financially hit the ceiling and through an ultimatum, desire a different type of return on their investment.

It's that **irrational** stance and insistence on changing the strip club game (theory) that sours the relationship between the Regular (patron) and the

Favorite (stripper).

Keep in mind, if anything evolves outside the strip club, it will happen naturally and not because of an ultimatum.

ECONOMIST NOTE

A Favorite (stripper) is the prize possession in a strip club. She's one-of-a-kind, providing the 'Bang' and the best overall return on one's investment. And as her Regular (patron), those returns increase over time.

LAW
18

TRICKLE-DOWN ECONOMICS

He'll call that trickle-down. I call it Niagara Falls.

—Jack Kemp

In political arenas and economic forums, one of the most popular terms you'll hear is the catchphrase "trickle-down economics." It refers to the enticing theory that if you reduce the taxes of the super wealthy and business owners of the world, that surplus of capital will be invested right back into the growth of the economy and eventually trickle-down to the average hardworking citizen.

Sounds good, right?

But in reality, it's an unproven theory that

catches the ear because it plays on the optimism of the general public and their hopes for prosperity.

Only in strip club economics is the trickle-down theory a proven concept. Tipping is a *real* investment. Whether you "Make It Drizzle" or you "Make It Rain," tipping stimulates the strip club economy and increases the stripper's bag. In particular, those **trickles** (tips) allow the stripper to make short-term and long-term investments into her brand. And if you decide to become an angel investor, sponsor or a venture capitalist and **trickle** a considerable amount of tips into one stripper—preferably your Favorite (stripper)—that builds real value called **stripper equity**.

Stripper Equity is defined as:

The amount of interest (time and money) invested into a stripper with the expectation of return.

It's important to choose wisely and invest in the right stripper's brand, and watch the trickle-down increase the supply of the strip club fantasy. The capital gains yielded will be worth every visit. The return on your investment (ROI) will keep you in VIP.

ECONOMIST NOTE

Only in strip club economics is the trickle-down theory a proven concept. Every trickle (tip) stimulates the strip club economy and increases the stripper's bag.

LAW 19

URBAN STRIP CLUB ECONOMICS

Within strip club economics, there is a branch of study that focuses strictly on strip clubs in urban areas that are heavily influenced by hip-hop culture and its promotion of the house party/after-party lifestyle: **Urban Strip Club Economics**.

In leading strip club cities like Atlanta, Houston, Dallas, Chicago, Los Angeles, and Miami, urban strip clubs have long set the benchmark on niche marketing, style, and culture. Unlike the Cheetahs, Spearmint Rhino's, and Déjà Vu's of the world, urban strip clubs provide a different type of strip club experience. The urban 'strip club fantasy' is more like a walkthrough on the set of a superstar rapper's music video. The strippers are the video vixens, twerking and looking sexy. And of course, the song is a strip club anthem about 'making it rain' and celebrating life and immediate success.

THE FIVE MAIN CHARACTERISTICS OF URBAN STRIP CLUB ECONOMICS

- **Value System**: Urban strip clubs have a different value system from classical strip clubs. The urban strip club experience is similar to a packed house party and strippers happened to show up. The main attraction is the party and the partygoer, not the stripper and the private dance.
- **The Rapper Theory**: The urban strip club is where the rapper theory and the "Make It Rain" movement started. Although the rapper theory is critical on impressionable patrons, the rapper's influence on strip club culture is undeniable and not possible without the urban strip club.
- **Influence of Hip-Hop Culture**: The DJ in the urban strip club plays a wide variety of hip-hop songs and never misses the chance to play a classic strip club anthem.
- **The Stage Dance**: Strippers in urban strip clubs present such a hypnotic stage dance full of twerking

and booty shaking that it rivals the lap dance in popularity and preference. Some patrons forget all about the lap dance.

- **Social Media**: Compared to classical and neoclassical strip clubs, the use of social media by patrons is allowed and more often encouraged in urban strip clubs. They cater to patrons who value the exposure and the pursuit of strip club fame. Discretion and privacy are old concepts.

The **Strip Club Economist** knows the clear difference between a classical strip club, a neoclassical strip club, and an urban strip club. The latter provides a unique experience and a different type of strip club fantasy.

ECONOMIST NOTE

Urban Strip Club Economics is a unique branch of study that focuses on strip clubs that are heavily influenced by hip-hop culture and its "Make It Rain" policy.

LAW 20

UNDERGROUND ECONOMY

If you destroy a free market you create a black market.

—Winston Churchill

In traditional economics, the underground economy refers to illegal economic activity that happens outside the bounds of legality. But in strip club economics, the underground economy refers to the economic activity that lingers outside of the strip club.

In classical theory, when a strip club does not foster the relationship between a stripper and a patron, the strip club supply and demand curve is at a non-equilibrium. Failing to provide a capitalistic environment where the stripper can take advantage of her skills and services, has its ramifications. Those failures open up the opportunity for the underground economy to flourish and truth be told, it's always there waiting in the wings, ready to be exploited.

CHARACTERISTICS OF THE UNDERGROUND ECONOMY

- **Bachelor Parties**: These parties are staples in American culture, and when the money dries up, strippers are more apt to entertain a rowdy bunch of partygoers outside of the club.
- **Private Parties**: The private party circuit always heats up when the strip club supply and demand curve is at a non-equilibrium. Strippers start looking for other locations to provide the Bang and secure a bag.
- **Extracurricular Activity**: Use your imagination.

THE EFFECTS OF THE UNDERGROUND ECONOMY

The effects of an underground economy is a seedy, **black market** full of **shadow prices**, **'under the table transactions'** and **vices**. Drugs and pills appear on the food menu, and paper trails are burnt up with a cigarette lighter. Secrets and information become another form of currency.

When the business goes underground, supply and demand meet and discuss numbers on a slanted curve. The effects can be extremely profitable or catastrophic.

ECONOMIST NOTE

When the strip club environment fails to connect supply and demand between the stripper and the patron, the underground economy is always there in the dark waiting to take advantage.

LAW
21

ARE YOU A STRIP CLUB ECONOMIST?

An economist is a man who states the obvious in terms of the incomprehensible.

—Alfred A. Knopf

After you digest Laws 1-20 and thoroughly understand the concepts, you must now ask yourself "Are you a strip club economist?"

Do you see things from a Macro and Micro point of view?

The PH.D. program only accepts applicants with the right mentality and those who are ready to do the fieldwork. Here's your checklist:

A strip club economist is ***rational.***
A strip club economist is a critical thinker.
A strip club economist acts in their own self-interest.
A strip club economist knows why they enter the strip club.
A strip club economist does not chase strip club fame.
A strip club economist is not a groupie for celebrities and rappers.
A strip club economist respects the stripper's hustle.
A strip club economist knows that the stripper is the main attraction.
A strip club economist understands the need for discretion and privacy.
A strip club economist is strategic with distributing their resources (time and money).
A strip club economist upholds the strip club hierarchy: Stripper > Waitress > Bartender.

If you resonate with the principles above, then you are ready to carry the title of **Strip Club Economist** and play the strip club game (theory) with a new sense of economic clarity and analysis.

ECONOMIST NOTE

Do you think you have what it takes to be a Strip Club Economist? The PH.D. program requires you to adhere to certain characteristics and principles.

THE STRIP CLUB SUPPLY AND DEMAND CURVE

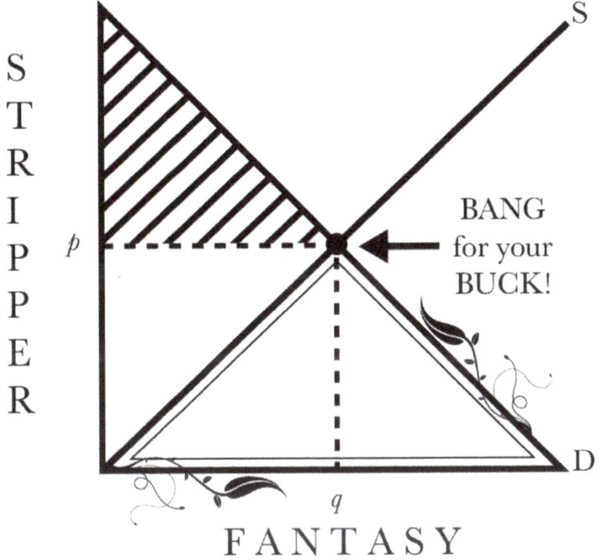

THE STRIPPER SUPPLIES THE FANTASY AT A PRICE...
THE PATRON DEMANDS THE FANTASY TO NEVER END AT A COST...
IN VIP IS WHERE THE EQUILIBRIUM MEETS WITH A BANG!

GLOSSARY

THE LANGUAGE OF STRIP CLUB ECONOMICS

BANG FOR YOUR BUCK: A phrase that means the patron got their 'money's worth' and their thirst was quenched, albeit temporarily. The BANG in the phrase 'Bang for your Buck' is the immediate: Benefit Acquired Not including Gratuity.

THE BARE MARKET: The economic market within the strip club that is dominated and controlled by the stripper and her monopolistic power to bare it all in more ways than one.

THE BLACK MARKET: Within the underground economy, the black market is the seedy market that's ripe with drugs, vices, 'under the table transactions 'and extracurricular activity.

THE CLASSICAL THEORY: The fundamental principle of the classical theory is that the sole purpose to visit a strip club is to interact (mentality, physically and financially) with the one and only, main attraction: the stripper.

EXTRACURRICULAR ACTIVITY: Use your imagination.

FAVORITE: 1. A patron's favorite stripper. Although a patron may claim to have several, only one will receive the majority of the patron's resources (time and money). 2. A Favorite is one of the two halves of the socioeconomic union that makes up the core foundation of the strip club industry. The supply and demand relationship between a Favorite (stripper) and a Regular (patron) provides the money flow that supports the entire strip club economy.

INCENTIVE: The primary motivation to enter a strip club and interact (mentality, physically, and financially) with a stripper.

THE INVISIBLE HAND: The invisible force that guides the strip club game (theory), helping supply and demand connect and reach equilibrium.

IRRATIONAL BEHAVIOR: A patron who enters a strip club to treat the one and only main attraction, the stripper, as a secondary source of entertainment or a sideshow.

LAISSEZ-FAIRE: A French term that means to "let go." In strip club economics, laissez-faire means to 'Let go, and the strip club game (theory) will take care of itself."

LAW OF DIMINISHING RETURNS: A law that states that if a patron doesn't find a Favorite (stripper) and become her Regular (patron), they will always be subject to a stripper that provides a strip club fantasy that eventually diminishes in quality and quantity.

LAW OF INCREASING RETURNS: The law of increasing returns is the opposite of the law of diminishing returns. The law states that if a patron can find a true

Favorite (stripper) to invest in and become her Regular (patron)—although the cost doesn't diminish—the return on the investment increases on every visit.

MACRO (INDUSTRY) ECONOMICS: The branch of strip club economics that focuses on the 'big picture', the overall business aspect of the industry as a whole.

MICRO (G-STRING) ECONOMICS: The branch of strip club economics that focuses on the 'small picture', the behavior, the decision making and the one-on-one interactions between the stripper and the patron.

MONOPOLY: The exclusive, controlling power that the stripper holds on the lap dance market.

THE NEOCLASSICAL THEORY: The fundamental principle of the neoclassical theory is that the only way modern-day strip clubs can compete in an oversaturated market is to take a multi-purpose, all-encompassing, buffet-style entertainment approach to an otherwise classical business model.

THE PATRON'S DILEMMA: Unlike the imaginary Prisoner's Dilemma used in the economics of game theory, the Patron's Dilemma is a real-life situation that exposes the challenges that come with choosing the right stripper and getting the most 'Bang for your Buck' in the strip club game (theory).

THE PATRON'S HIERARCHY OF NEEDS: The motivational theory that everything flows and revolves around the three-level pyramid of services. The coveted lap dance is at the top of the hierarchy of needs; followed by the table dance and lastly the stage dance. The three levels enable the patron to utilize their five senses (sight, hearing, smell, touch, and taste) to their maximum.

PURE COMPETITION: A term that describes a market that is filled with aggressive competitors who are selling the same product and service.

THE RAPPER THEORY: The fundamental principle of the rapper theory is that the superstar rapper, for better or worse, has strongly influenced patron behavior and indirectly modified strip club etiquette.

RATIONAL BEHAVIOR: A patron who knows that the sole purpose of entering a strip club is to interact (mentality, physically, and financially) with the one and only main attraction, the stripper. Everything else is secondary and a convenient distraction from that fact.

REGULAR: 1. A regular is a patron who frequents the strip club; a recognizable face that is familiar with the environment and staff. 2. Formerly considered a negative label (some consider being a Regular a pathetic loser), a Regular is one of the two halves of the socioeconomic union that makes up the core foundation of the strip club industry. The supply and demand relationship between a Favorite (stripper) and a Regular (patron) provides the money flow that supports the entire strip club economy.

RETURN ON INVESTMENT (ROI): The amount of engagement, intimacy and cooperation received after investing time and money into a stripper.

SCARCITY: The fact that although patrons have unlimited thirst for T and A, they also have a limited amount of resources, and a finite number of strippers that can (temporarily) quench that thirst and provide the ultimate Strip Club Fantasy.

SHADOW PRICE: A price that is discussed in the shadows of the black market.

STRIP CLUB ECONOMICS: The study of behavior and choice in a strip club environment fueled by money and governed by two determining factors: thirst and scarcity.

STRIP CLUB ECONOMIST: A rational thinking patron who approaches the strip club game (theory) with an economic point of view and has thoroughly digested *The 21 Laws of Strip Club Economics* and its principles.

STRIP CLUB FANTASY: A unique entertainment bundle that is only provided by a stripper and solely experienced at a strip club.

THE STRIP CLUB GAME (THEORY): The observation and study of how patrons and strippers behave and interact strategically in a strip club environment fueled by money and influenced by self-interest, motives, and agendas. Each participant is playing to win advantage and position.

THE STRIP CLUB SUPPLY AND DEMAND CURVE: A simple economic model of price determination used to analyze and visualize the strip club's free-market at work, through the fundamental relationship between supply and demand.

STRIPPER EQUITY: The amount of interest (time and money) invested into a stripper with the expectation of return.

THERE'S NO SUCH THING AS A FREE TOUCH (TNSTAAFT): A timeless strip club adage that highlights the fact that nothing is free. Everything has a cost, whether hidden, visible or verbally communicated.

THIRST: The Hasty Instinctual Reaction to Sexual Tantalization.

TRICKLE-DOWN ECONOMICS: The theory based on the reality that within the strip club, the tips given by patrons actually do trickle-down and increase the stripper's bag and create stimuli throughout the strip club economy.

UNDERGROUND ECONOMY: Economic activity that happens outside of the strip club.

URBAN STRIP CLUB ECONOMICS: The branch of strip club economics that focuses strictly on strip clubs in urban areas that are heavily influenced by hip-hop culture and its promotion of the house party/after-party lifestyle.

BIBLIOGRAPHY

Barkley, Andrew. *The Economics of Food and Agricultural Markets:* New Prairie Press., 2016

"Bizfluent." *Bizfluent,* www.bizfluent.com/.

The Economics Book: DK Pub., 2012.

Debertin, David L. *Agricultural Production Economics (Second Edition):* Amazon Createspace, 2012

"Economics Help." *Economics Help,* www.econmichelp.org

"Economist." *Wikipedia,* Wikimedia Foundation, 7 Mar. 2019, en.wikipedia.org/wiki/Economist.

"Essay on Economics." Economics Discussion, 2 Feb. 2016, www.economicsdiscussion.net/essays/economics/essay-on-economics/17671.

"Explore Encyclopedia Britannica." *Encyclopedia Britannica,* Encyclopedia Britannica, Inc., www.britannica.com/.

OpenStax. "Principles of Economics." *Principles of Economics,* opentextbc.ca/princplesofeconomics/.

"Sharper Insight. Smarter Investing." *Investopedia,* Investopedia, www.investopedia.com/.

wikiHow. "How to Become an Economist." *WikiHow,* WikiHow, 8

Apr. 2019, www.wikihow.com/Become-an-Economist.

Thompson, Derek. "The Irrational Consumer: Why Economics Is Dead Wrong About How We Make Choices." *The Atlantic*, Atlantic Media Company, 16 Jan. 2013, www.theatlantic.com/business/archive/2013/01/the-irrational-consumer-why-economics-is-dead-wrong-about-how-we-make-choices/267255/

"World News, Politics, Economics, Business & Finance." *The Economist*, The Economist Newspaper, www.economist.com/.

INDEX

H

I

L

M

N

O

P

R

www.ingramcontent.com/pod-product-compliance
Lightning Source LLC
LaVergne TN
LVHW051938100826
845154LV00016B/164/J

* 9 7 8 0 9 9 7 4 3 2 0 9 1 *